A Picnic at Sunset

Explorer Challenge

What is Chip pointing at?

OXFORD
UNIVERSITY PRESS

The sky was red.

Mum ran to get the camera.

Mum ran back to the top of
the cliff.

Oh no! The camera was not in
the bag.

Mum ran back.

Was the camera lost?

No! Dad had it in his pocket.

Oh no! The sun had set.

Retell the Story

Look at the pictures and retell the story in your own words.

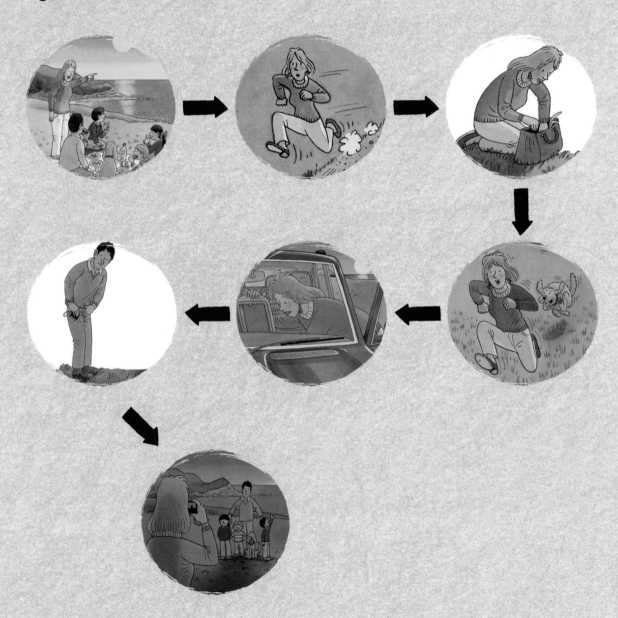

Look Back, Explorers

What colour was the sky?

Where was the camera?

How do you think Mum felt when she couldn't find the camera?

Did you find out what Chip was pointing at?

What's Next, Explorers?

Now read about what some animals do when the sun sets ...

Explorer Challenge
for *At Sunset*

Who rests upside down?